EXPLORING EARTH'S · BIOMES ·

OCEAN

APRIL PULLEY SAYRE

TF
CB

TWENTY-FIRST CENTURY BOOKS

A Division of Henry Holt and Company
• New York •

For Candace and the ocean,
both powerful and nurturing

ACKNOWLEDGMENTS

Our thanks to the following experts who reviewed portions of this manuscript: Michael Rigsby of the Monterey Bay Aquarium, and Ellen M. Peel, special counsel for living marine resources, Center for Marine Conservation.

Twenty-First Century Books
A Division of Henry Holt and Company, Inc.
115 West 18th Street
New York, NY 10011

Henry Holt® and colophon are trademarks of
Henry Holt and Company, Inc.
Publishers since 1866

Library of Congress Cataloging-in-Publication Data
Sayre, April Pulley.
Ocean / April Pulley Sayre.—1st ed.
p. cm.—(Exploring earth's biomes)
Includes bibliographical references and index.
Summary: Describes the physical features of the ocean biome,
as well as ocean life, human use, and conservation efforts.
1. Ocean—Juvenile literature. [1. Ocean.] I. Title.
II. Series: Sayre, April Pulley. Exploring earth's biomes.
GC21.5.S29 1996
551.46—dc20   96-2419
                                                          CIP
                                                          AC

ISBN 0-8050-4084-6
First Edition—1996

Designed by Kelly Soong

Printed in Mexico
All first editions are printed on acid-free paper ∞.
1 3 5 7 9 10 8 6 4 2

Photo credits appear on page 80.

CONTENTS

INTRODUCTION TO AQUATIC BIOMES

The water that makes up more than two-thirds of your body weight, that flows in your blood, that bathes your cells, and that you cry as tears, may once have flowed in a river. It may have floated as a cloud, fallen as a snowflake, bobbed in ocean waves, or been drunk by a dinosaur from an ancient lake. All this is possible because the water that's presently on earth has always been here—except for ice brought by comets hitting the earth's atmosphere. And all the water on earth is connected in a global cycle. This cycle is called the water cycle, or the hydrologic cycle.

Every day, all over the earth, water exists in and moves through this cycle. Ninety-seven percent of the earth's water is in the oceans. Two percent is in frozen glaciers and ice caps at the Poles. The remaining 1 percent is divided among the world's lakes, rivers, groundwater, soil moisture, and water vapor in the air. All this comes to a grand total of 326 million cubic miles (1,359 million cubic kilometers) of water. Every day, this water is exchanged among the oceans, streams, clouds, glaciers, lakes, wetlands, and even dew-covered leaves. Even now, it is being exhaled from your body, as moisture in your breath.

As the water cycles, at times it changes phase from solid to liquid to gas. The heat of the sun warms water on the land's surface, in lakes, in streams, in the ocean, even on the leaves of plants—and causes this water to evaporate, to turn into a gas. This gas rises into the air, cools, and condenses, eventually forming clouds and falling back to earth as liquid rain or solid snow or hail. This precipitation makes its way into streams, rivers, lakes, oceans, glaciers, and ice caps, and underground. And so the cycle continues. But it's not quite so simple. Each portion of the cycle is connected to others. For example, river water runs into oceans, stream water runs into lakes, and water from underground bubbles out of springs and into rivers. Water is constantly being exchanged among all the many places it resides on planet earth.

Almost anywhere water exists as a liquid, it is colonized by organisms—bacteria, amoebas, fungi, animals, or plants. Some watery habitats have particular physical conditions and particular kinds of plants and animals inhabiting them. These are aquatic biomes: ocean, river, lake, and coral reef. Where these aquatic biomes mingle with terrestrial, or land, biomes, they may form special, semiaquatic, fringe communities. Wetland and seashore are two of these communities that are unique enough and widespread enough to qualify as major biomes.

All aquatic and semiaquatic biomes—ocean, river, lake, coral reef, seashore, and wetland—are influenced by regional climate and the lands nearby. These biomes are also linked to one another, by ever-moving water molecules and the global water cycle through which they flow.

§ 1 §
THE OCEAN
BIOME

If you look down at our planet from outer space, you might decide to name it Ocean instead of Earth. Most of what you see—71 percent of the planet's surface—is covered by ocean, not land. In the ocean, turtles dive, lobsters walk, fish school, coral reefs grow, and comb jellies glow in the dark. Icebergs as big as cities float in the ocean.

Certainly, the ocean is a place of superlatives: the world's biggest living animal—the blue whale; the tallest peak—Mauna Kea; the longest mountain range—the mid-Atlantic ridge. But the ocean's importance reaches beyond mind-boggling statistics because it interacts with the atmosphere to control living conditions all over the earth. Ocean currents can affect wide-ranging events, from snowfall in the Rockies to drought in southern Africa. They play a major role in determining both weather and climate worldwide.

Like desert and grassland, ocean is a biome—an area that has a certain kind of community of animals and plants. But unlike terrestrial—land—biomes, ocean does not have a characteristic climate. Ocean occurs throughout the world, extending from chilly polar regions to hot tropical shores. And ocean life, although affected by climate, is in-

Seen from space, the earth is clearly an ocean planet, with much more water than land.

fluenced just as much by oceanic factors such as currents, waves, tides, temperature, salinity, and depth.

Most of the ocean—about 80 percent of its surface area—is located in the Southern Hemisphere. The Northern Hemisphere, in contrast, contains most of the earth's land and only 20 percent of the world's ocean. The ocean that wraps the globe is divided into four major regions: the Atlantic Ocean, the Pacific Ocean, the Indian Ocean, and the Arctic Ocean. (Some geographers consider the waters around Antarctica to be a separate, fifth ocean, as well.) These oceans, although distinct in some ways, are interconnected; ocean water circulates among them all.

The world's ocean is a uniquely global resource. It laps the shores of many countries. Ships traveling across its surface transport people and materials worldwide. Fish and shrimp caught in its waters show up on dinner tables from Georgia to Japan. Medicines, minerals, and oil harvested from its waters and the ocean floor are used in countries from Argentina to Austria. Managing the demand for the ocean's many bounties as human population grows will likely be one of the biggest challenges of the next century.

DIVISIONS

Oceanographers divide the ocean into three main layers:

- The sunlit (epipelagic) zone—the top layer of the ocean, where enough sunlight penetrates for plants to carry on photosynthesis.
- The twilight (mesopelagic) zone—a dim zone where some light penetrates, but not enough for plants to grow.
- The midnight (bathypelagic) zone—the deep ocean layer where no light penetrates.

The deepest portions of the oceans have additional layers called the abyssal zone and the hadal zone.

PHYSICAL FEATURES

- Ocean water is salty and, in general, cold. Most ocean water is less than 36°F (2.2°C). But in the Tropics, surface water may reach 82°F (28°C), and water can be much hotter near underwater volcanoes. Unlike most land biomes, the ocean's temperature varies very little day to day in any given spot.
- Oceans have tides—a periodic rise and fall of water levels. These are most noticeable along seashores.
- Ocean waters are constantly in motion because of waves, tides, and currents—large amounts of water that travel long distances, like rivers in the ocean.
- The weight of water pressing down from above makes pressure very high at ocean depths.
- The ocean bottom is 2.3 miles (3.7 kilometers) deep on average, but 6.85 miles (11 kilometers) deep at its lowest point, in the Mariana Trench in the Pacific.

ANIMALS

- Animals that live in the ocean are called marine animals. (Ocean plants are called marine plants.)
- The ocean has favorable conditions for life. Organisms live throughout the ocean, from its surface to its greatest depths.
- Ocean life is "patchy." One area may be packed with animals and plants while nearby areas may be almost empty.
- Ocean animals are highly diverse. Many phyla—major scientific groups—of animals exist only in the ocean and not on land.
- Water's buoyancy supports the bodies of many ocean creatures, such as jellyfish, which could not survive on land.
- Ocean organisms are divided into three groups: plankton—those that float; nekton—those that actively swim; and benthos—those that live on or in the ocean bottom.

PLANTS

- Phytoplankton—tiny, often microscopic floating plants— are the main ocean plants.
- Ocean plants can gain the minerals and water they need directly from seawater.
- Plants, including phytoplankton, can only live in shallow waters and near the surface of the ocean, where sunlight is available.
- In shallows, seaweeds attach to the ocean floor.

§ 2 §
THE WORLD'S OCEANS

Open up an atlas and look at a map. But this time, ignore the land; look at the ocean instead. Run your fingers over a contoured globe and discover the rippled ridges, valleys, and mountains of the ocean floor. Begin seeing the ocean, not as an edge of the land, but as the dominant feature of planet earth. Oceanographers—scientists who study the ocean—see the ocean in just this way.

OCEAN WORDS, OCEAN WORLDS

The words *ocean* and *sea* are often used interchangeably. But for oceanographers these words have more specific meanings. Oceans are the earth's largest uninterrupted expanses of water. The earth's four oceans are the Pacific, the Atlantic, the Indian, and the Arctic Oceans. (The waters surrounding the continent of Antarctica are considered a separate ocean by some scientists.)

Seas, in contrast, are smaller lobes of the ocean that are partly surrounded by land. (Confusingly, some huge inland lakes such as the Caspian Sea are called seas as well.) The world's seas include the Arabian Sea, the North Sea, the Mediterranean Sea, the Philippine Sea, the Coral Sea, and the Bering Sea, among others. Even though oceans and seas are different, some general ocean words still contain the word *sea*. Seawater, sea level, seascape, and other terms refer to features of both ocean and sea.

THE FOUR OCEANS

Three world oceans—the Atlantic, the Pacific, and the Indian—are bounded on the south by Antarctica. Two of these, the Atlantic and Pacific, extend north from Antarctica all the way to the Arctic Ocean. These tremendous oceans encompass chilly polar waters as well as warm tropical shores and coral reefs. Their smaller cousin, the Indian Ocean, hugs the underside of Asia. The Indian Ocean encompasses tropical islands but also meets icy waters where it borders Antarctica. The fourth ocean, the Arctic Ocean, is cold throughout. It's a partially frozen ice cap atop the world.

Pacific Ocean

SURFACE AREA: 64,000,000 square miles
(166,000,000 square kilometers)
AVERAGE DEPTH: 13,737 feet (4,188 meters)

The Pacific is the largest and deepest ocean, stretching from California to Japan, and from Alaska to Antarctica. It contains half of all the ocean surface area on earth. (That's more surface area than all of the earth's land combined!) The Pacific Ocean holds roughly twice as much water as the Atlantic Ocean. Yet strangely, only one-seventh of the world's river water runs into this ocean, despite its massive size.

Roughly rounded in shape, the Pacific Ocean touches five continents: North America, South America, Antarctica, Australia, and Eurasia. Its floor is scarred by numerous trenches and it is peppered with islands on its western side. On that side, the ocean extends into numerous curved lobes: the Bering Sea, the Sea of Okhotsk, the Sea of Japan,

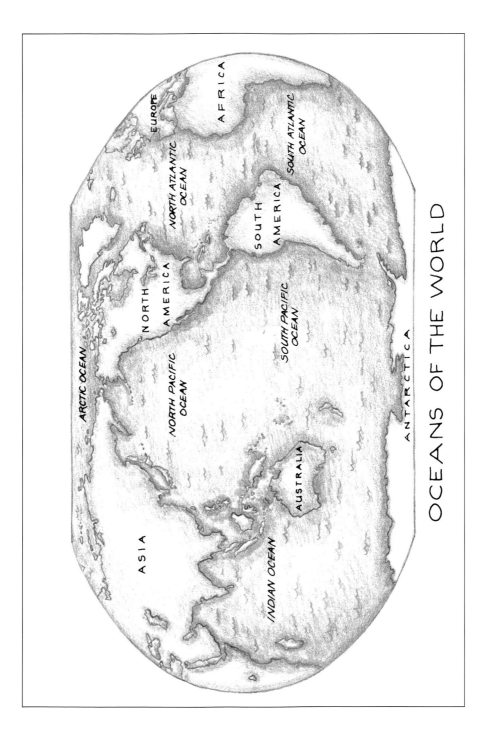

OCEANS OF THE WORLD

13

the Yellow Sea, the East China Sea, and the South China Sea. Chains of undersea mountains reach up from its floor to form islands, including Japan.

On its eastern side, the Pacific runs along North and South America in a relatively unbroken seam. This seam is a volcanically active one, however, as the continents press westward against the ocean floor. This has caused the land to wrinkle into coastal mountains, including South America's famed Andes Mountains. Volcanic activity is so common around the edges of the Pacific that people call its borders the Ring of Fire. Part of this Ring of Fire is the east Pacific rise—a wide ridge that is part of the global system of seams, where pieces of the earth's crust meet.

The Pacific Ocean is so vast that it contains a wide variety of marine life and habitats. Off California and Peru are kelp forests—underwater forests of seaweed where sea otters frolic and feed. Near Peru, anchovies thrive in mind-boggling numbers, supporting a rich fishing industry. In the west-central Pacific, coral reefs abound, supporting colorful reef fish, turtles, manta rays, and sharks. Near Antarctica, blue whales feed, gulping down krill by the ton. At the opposite end of the Pacific, fishers and orcas compete for fat salmon making their way toward Alaska's rivers to spawn.

Atlantic Ocean

SURFACE AREA: 31,660,000 square miles
              (82,000,000 square kilometers)
AVERAGE DEPTH: 10,930 feet (3,330 meters)

The Atlantic Ocean is the second largest ocean in the world. In the Northern Hemisphere, it is sandwiched between North America and Europe. In the Southern Hemisphere, it divides South America from Africa.

Down the Atlantic's center, running generally north to south, is a ridge like a backbone, with a deep trench in its center. This is the mid-Atlantic ridge—the birthplace of the floor of the Atlantic Ocean. It's where molten rock oozes up to form ocean floor. The mid-Atlantic ridge curves like a snake, and the ocean's edges curve parallel to it. Crossing the ridge are fracture zones. These zones are deep, geologically active valleys where earthquakes and volcanic activity are common. The deepest spot in this ocean is in the Puerto Rico Trench, at 30,184 feet (9,200 meters) deep.

The Atlantic Ocean has rich fisheries, particularly off the coasts of New England and Newfoundland. This area is a busy shipping region for traffic from Europe to North and South America and back. The Atlantic Ocean has a variety of habitats. The Caribbean Sea is a warm spot, with numerous small islands with coral reefs. In the central North

An amazing variety of penguins can be found in the South Atlantic. Here, a Gentoo penguin feeds its chicks.

Atlantic are the clear waters of the Sargasso Sea, where sargasso weed floats and eels reproduce. Ocean life abounds in the Atlantic, with the full range of marine animals, from the penguins of the South Atlantic to the sea turtles and manatees of the Caribbean to the whales that migrate through great expanses of the ocean.

Indian Ocean

SURFACE AREA: 24,400,000 square miles
              (63,400,000 square kilometers)
AVERAGE DEPTH: 12,760 feet (3,890 meters)

The world's third largest ocean, the Indian Ocean, hugs the underside of Asia, in between Africa and Australia. It extends into the Arabian Sea and the Bay of Bengal, which sit on each side of India. In those regions the ocean floor is loaded with sediment dropped by the Indus River and the Ganges River. The major geologic feature of the Indian Ocean is an underwater mountain chain—a forked ridge that's shaped like an upside-down Y. This ridge begins where the mid-Atlantic ridge curves under Africa. It continues northward, "pointing" toward the Red Sea. Then it runs southward and below Australia, where it meets the Antarctic ridge.

Much of the Indian Ocean lies in the Tropics. It contains coral reefs around islands and mangrove swamps along shorelines. Squid, flying fish, colorful reef fish, sharks, and sea turtles inhabit these waters. The dugong, a rare, larger relative of the manatee, nibbles plants in warm shallows close to shore. In tropical areas, surface water can be warm, as warm as 82°F (28°C) in the Bay of Bengal in summer. But near Antarctica, waters can be as cold as 30°F (-1°C)! Penguins, seals, and whales feed on krill and fish in these chilly waters.

16

The dugong — a mammal — is an endangered species.
It is related to the manatee, which is also endangered.

Arctic Ocean

SURFACE AREA: 4,700,000 square miles
(12,173,000 square kilometers)
AVERAGE DEPTH: 3,250 feet (990 meters)

Bounded by the northern edges of Eurasia and North America, the Arctic Ocean is small, generally shallow, and very cold. It is ice covered much of the year. Pack ice—the ocean's icy shell—floats in pieces on the ocean's top. These ice floes drift, split apart, unfreeze and refreeze, and even crash into one another, making earsplitting noise. In winter, when the ocean is completely frozen over, polar bears, wolves, and people can walk on the ice, crossing the ocean on foot.

Much of the exploration of the Arctic Ocean was motivated by the search for a Northwest Passage—an easy shortcut from Europe to the Far East. European merchants wanted a faster, better route for gathering valuable Chinese and Indian silks and spices. Beginning around 1500, this search for a new route inspired numerous expeditions. One group of explorers, their ship frozen into the ice, drifted for almost three years. It was not until 1906 that a ship made the entire voyage; that trip took three years. The Northwest Passage is one "easy shortcut" that's turned out to be neither short nor easy at all!

During the dark arctic winters, this ocean's plants are inactive—they do not grow. Even when it gets lighter, a thick icy covering prevents light from reaching tiny floating marine plants. But in spring, when much of the ice melts, the plants grow rapidly and multiply, creating a smorgasbord of food. Fish, seals, whales, dolphins, and walruses feed on the resulting feast. The narwhal also lives in these waters. It is a seal-like creature with a long, twisted horn that may have inspired tales of unicorns in days gone by.

§ 3 §
PHYSICAL FEATURES
OF OCEANS

In May 1990, 62,000 Nike tennis shoes fell off a ship southeast of Alaska. Nine months later, some of the shoes started appearing on the coasts of British Columbia, Washington State, and Oregon. Beachcombers picked up shoes by the hundreds, even holding swap meets to assemble usable matched pairs. For oceanographers, the shipping disaster had an unexpected payoff: information on ocean currents. Where the shoes end up—some are still drifting—will give scientists new clues about how currents behave. Currents are just one of the ocean's many physical features that still puzzle scientists.

OCEAN WATER

If you put ocean water in a shallow pan and let the water evaporate, a white crust of salt will be left behind. Much of this salt is sodium chloride—the same salt used in food. About a third of the world's table salt is mined from the ocean using a similar technique. Eighty other chemicals, including magnesium, calcium, and potassium, are found in ocean water, as well. Seawater even contains silver and gold. Don't start collecting bucketsful to make your fortune, though. The silver and gold exist in only minuscule amounts!

Salt Starts   Where does the ocean get its salt? From rivers and runoff—water flowing off the land. This water, flowing across rocks and through soil, dissolves natural salts and carries them to the ocean. Other salts come from gases emitted by underwater volcanoes and deep-sea rifts. Once dissolved in ocean water, salts circulate through the ocean, or they may deposit as particles on the ocean floor. Remarkably, ocean salt also plays a role in making rain. As ocean waves break, they splash salt into the air, creating atmospheric dust. This salty dust forms nuclei on which water can collect, forming ice crystals and rain.

Cold as Ice   Whales have blubber and people wear wet suits for good reason: to stay warm in the ocean. The ocean, in general, is cold, about 36°F (2.2°C). Water near Antarctica can even be 28°F (-2.2°C), which is colder than ice. (Seawater doesn't freeze at that temperature because it's so salty.) At the other extreme, ocean water can be hot: over 500°F (260°C) near hydrothermal vents, where water percolates through volcanically heated rock. But these hot spots are the exception. The ocean is still relatively cold, especially deep down. In the sunny Tropics, coastal surface waters may heat up to 86°F (30°C); but offshore, deep-ocean water remains cold.

Under Pressure   If you dive down in a lake or swimming pool, you may find your ears begin to hurt. Water pressure is the reason. Deep in a pool, lake, or ocean, the weight of the water above compresses the water below. The water compresses other things, too—animals, people, and oxygen bubbles. Scuba divers have to learn how to equalize the pressure in their ears to avoid injuring them when they dive. Deep-ocean creatures must cope with this crushing pressure year-round.

*A wet suit can
help a scuba diver
conserve body heat.*

WATCH THAT PRESSURE!

The deeper you go in the ocean, the higher the water pressure. In this activity you'll see that water pressure is high at the bottom of *any* water column.

Materials you will need:
- A tall, cylindrical can. (A large juice can, 46 fluid ounces [1.36 liters] works well. A coffee can also works well. But any medium- to large-sized can will do.)
- A ruler
- A nail
- A hammer
- Masking tape
- Water
- A large sink in which to work. (Any place that can

get wet will work. You can do the demonstration outdoors if you like.)

1. With an adult's supervision, use the hammer and nail to make a row of four holes in the side of the can. First, measure about an inch from the bottom of the can. Lay the can on its side. Hammer the nail into the can until it makes a hole. Pull out the nail. Repeat this action to make same-sized holes two, three, and four inches from the bottom of the can.
2. Cover each of the holes with masking tape.
3. Place the can in a sink. Fill the can with water. (It's okay if some water leaks from the taped holes.)
4. Pull the tape off the holes.
5. Observe the water squirting out of the holes. Notice where the streams of water touch the sink. Which stream of water squirts the farthest away from the can? The one that squirts the farthest from the can is under the most pressure.

THE OCEAN'S MOTION

Every day, the ocean is in motion. Waves crash. Tides rise and fall. Currents carry drifting animals thousands of miles.

Making Waves When wind blows over the ocean's surface, it creates waves. Their size depends on how far, how fast, and how long the wind blows. Strong, steady winds over long distances create large waves. But giant waves, called tsunamis, are created by underwater earthquakes and landslides. These devastating waves can be 100 feet (30 meters) tall! Even when you feel no wind at all, you may encounter large swells created by distant storms. Swells are waves that change as they travel, becoming smooth, wide, gently sloping waves. When one passes, the ocean seems to swell, buoying a ship up, then gently placing it down.

Going With the Tide   Every day, water levels rise, then fall, along the earth's shorelines. These movements are the ocean's tides. On average, the difference between high and low tide is only a few feet. But in the Bay of Fundy, between Maine and Nova Scotia, the tide levels vary by 43 feet (13 meters)! Seashores experience one to two low tides and one to two high tides every 24 hours and 50 minutes. Tides are caused primarily by the gravitational attraction the moon and sun have for the earth's oceans. This attraction combines with the earth's spin to create traveling bulges of water—one on the side of the earth near the moon and one on the far side of the earth. As the moon circles the earth, it pulls these bulges along. So water levels vary as the bulges travel. These factors, plus the shape and steepness of coastal regions, make tides vary in height from day to day and place to place.

Currents on the Move   What helps tuna travel and freighter captains save fuel? Ocean currents. Tuna and sailors follow them. An ocean current is like a river of water that moves through the ocean. It can carry cold water to warm regions, or warm water to cold seas. Unlike waves, currents actually transport water long distances. (After a wave passes by, the water molecules return to about the same position in the ocean.) Most surface currents are caused by prevailing winds—strong winds that blow for long periods of time. The direction a current flows is also affected by the position of islands and continents and the rotation of the earth. Furthermore, as the earth spins, water tends to move to the right in the Northern Hemisphere and to the left in the Southern Hemisphere.

The Great Circles   In every ocean, surface currents travel in immense circles, called gyres. The gyres in the Northern Hemisphere run clockwise. Those in the Southern Hemisphere run counterclockwise. In the North Atlantic, the water traces a circular path thousands of miles wide, from Florida to Massachusetts to Spain to Cuba and back. The Pacific and Atlantic Oceans have two gyres each: one in the north, one in the south. The Indian Ocean has one, and so does the Arctic. The Antarctic continent has a current that circles it like a moat.

That Sinking Feeling   Some currents are not created by wind. They're caused by differences in water density. (Density is how closely packed the molecules in a substance are.) Cold water is dense, so it tends to sink below warmer water, which is less dense. Very salty water is also dense, so it tends to sink, too. In Antarctica, tremendous amounts of salty, cold water form as icebergs freeze and unfreeze. This dense water sinks down deep and spreads, traveling throughout the bottom of oceans worldwide. This moving mass of cold water is a deep-water current.

· THE TRAVELING SHOES ·

After the Nike shoe spill of 1990, oceanographers began recording where the shoes were found. The first shoes were found on the Pacific coast of North America. In 1993, some showed up in Hawaii. By 1996, some are expected to show up in the Philippines and Japan. Why? Because ocean currents circle the North Pacific, moving clockwise, in the North Pacific gyre. Carried in this gyre, the shoes could show up back on North American shores in 1997. Scientists are watching and looking for reports of the shoes to discover if their computer predictions are correct.

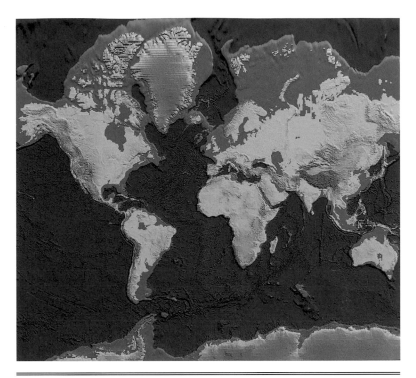

This topographical map shows the world's oceans in dark blue. Light blue areas are continental shelves.

OCEAN CONTOURS

The surface of the ocean may be relatively flat. But the ocean floor is not. Hidden under the waves are canyons, valleys, and even mountains—some taller than Mount Everest! Scientists divide the ocean floor into three major segments: the continental shelf, the continental slope, and the deep-ocean floor.

Shelf Space If you could walk out from a beach through the waves and underwater, you'd be walking on the continental shelf. This underwater edge of the continent slopes slightly downward and varies in width. Off California, the

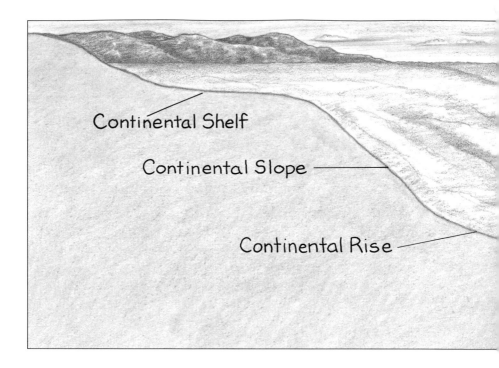

Continental Shelf

Continental Slope

Continental Rise

shelf drops away just offshore. Yet near Siberia, the shelf extends 1,100 miles (1,774 kilometers) from the land's edge.

When sea levels were lower, rivers ran through some of these areas that are now underwater. Scuba divers can still see old riverbeds and canyons that wrinkle continental shelves. In waters about 600 feet (180 meters) deep, the ocean bottom begins to slope. This is where the continental shelf ends and the continental slope begins.

The Big Drop The continental slope is steeper than the continental shelf. In places, it slopes gently; in other places, it drops off in cliffs. Although generally sloped, this underwater terrain is as complex as what you see above water. Canyons, plateaus, gorges, mounds, and basins vary its contours. The slope reaches to depths of about 12,000 feet

Deep Ocean Floor (Abyssal Plain)

(3,600 meters). Close to the base of the continental slope is a gentle rise called the continental rise. Beyond this rise is the deep-ocean floor.

The Deep Ocean Most of the deep ocean covers abyssal plain—relatively flat or gently rolling ocean floor. Breaking up these plains are ridges, volcanic mountains, mountain ranges, and trenches—the peaks and valleys of the ocean realm. Most of the ocean is from 1.8 to 3.7 miles (3 to 6 kilometers) deep. The Mariana Trench, in the Pacific Ocean, is 6.85 miles (11 kilometers) deep!

World Without Soil The ocean bottom is not bare rock. Mud, sand, minerals, and silt wash off the land and cover the ocean floor. Other sediments are from the sea itself. In

the deep sea, minerals from the water crystallize out onto
the ocean floor. And shells of dead plankton build up over
millions of years to form sediments called calcareous ooze.

OCEAN ORIGINS

Two to three billion years ago, one ocean called Panthalassa
wrapped the earth. All the continents we know today were
connected in one huge continent called Pangaea. Then, 200
million years ago, Pangaea began breaking into continents
that slowly moved away from one another. These continents separated because they were riding on tectonic
plates—gigantic slabs of the earth's crust and upper man-
tle. These plates slip and slide over molten rock beneath.

Wherever the tectonic plates moved apart, molten
rock oozed up to form ocean floor. By this process, called
sea-floor spreading, the Atlantic Ocean formed as Eurasia

objects such as enemy submarines. This technique, and refinements of it, also helped map the ocean floor. A new world of underwater mountains, volcanoes, trenches, and plains was revealed by sonar.

Today satellite technology helps in the efforts to complete the map of the ocean floor. In 1978, the Seasat satellite orbited the earth, bouncing microwaves off the ocean's surface. This revealed the ocean's surface—the water—was not flat at all. It's full of subtle hills and valleys of water. Over trenches, the water dips slightly down, and over underwater mountains it forms a bump. Information from the Seasat satellite and similar instruments has also led to the discovery of even more trenches and mountains on the ocean floor.

and North America spread apart. (Even today, more ocean floor is forming as lava pushes up and out of the mid-Atlantic ridge.) By thirty-five million years ago, the continents and oceans were located roughly where they are today.

Bye, Bye, Europe In case you haven't noticed, Europe is getting farther from North America. The Atlantic Ocean is growing wider by more than 1 inch (2½ centimeters) each year. In fact, when Columbus crossed the Atlantic in 1492, it was approximately 22 yards (20 meters) narrower than it is today! As the world's tectonic plates shift, other changes are taking place. The Pacific Ocean, once the site of Panthalassa, is growing smaller in size every day. Meanwhile, in the Middle East, a new ocean is forming. The Red Sea is growing larger, year by year. Scientists predict that it will become an ocean as big as the Atlantic—in 200 million years or so!

Coming Apart at the Seams   When oceans grow wider, and new ocean floor forms, the old "extra" crust has to go somewhere. Some is pushed into wrinkles—mountains on sea and on land. In other places, tectonic plates beneath the ocean smash together and slide under one another. Plate edges melt to become molten rock. (At these edges, deep-ocean trenches and ridges may form.) All the pushing, pulling, and sliding along plate edges can cause earth-quakes and volcanic eruptions nearby. Continents may even warp and fold from the pressure, causing shorelines to rise and sink.

Rise and Fall   Over thousands of years, ocean levels have risen and fallen drastically. Ten thousand years ago, during the last ice age, much of the world's ocean was frozen in ice at the Poles. Sea level was lower. Parts of the continental shelf that are now underwater were dry land then. Later, as the earth's climate warmed, the ice caps melted. The ocean warmed and expanded. Both of these factors caused ocean levels to rise to the levels we see today. Most scientists believe the earth's climate is continuing to warm and that sea level will slowly rise in the next century.

"CURRENT" EVENTS

Just read the headlines. Floods in southern California. Heavy rains in Germany. Fisheries collapse in Peru. Igua-nas die in the Galápagos. Drought hits Indonesia and Aus-tralia. These seemingly unconnected events have a shared thread: they're linked to changes in ocean currents. Each day, the ocean and the atmosphere interact to produce the world's weather and climate. Every ten years or so, ocean currents shift for two years. They push warm Pacific waters eastward toward South America, in what is called an El Niño event.

In an El Niño year, near Peru, surface waters increase in temperature, and sea levels rise as much as 20 inches (50 centimeters). A cold, nutrient-rich current that usually supports an abundance of plant life and sea life nearby suddenly disappears. The fisheries collapse. Fishers go bankrupt. Seabirds die by the thousands or millions. Seaweed doesn't grow well, so Galapágos iguanas go hungry. And weather patterns change worldwide. These changes can bring heavy rains to southern California and drought to inland Peru and even Australia. In the late 1980s and early 1990s, El Niño events occurred more often than usual, causing many droughts and floods.

As El Niño proves, the ocean's physical conditions— temperature, currents, and salinity— can have wide-ranging impacts. The ocean, which is an integral part of the world's weather engine, stores both water and heat. Ocean water heated by the intense sun at the equator mixes with water in other parts of the world. It helps transfer heat from the Tropics to the Poles. Recognizing the importance of the ocean-weather connection, many scientists are studying it worldwide. But right now the exact cause of El Niño is unknown. And so far, scientists cannot predict exactly when it will occur.

§ 4 §
OCEAN LIFE: FROM THE SURFACE TO THE DEPTHS

In many ways, the ocean is an easier place to live than the land is. Drying out isn't a danger for animals living in ocean water. And water contains some of each nutrient plants need. In addition, ocean water circulates, bringing food and taking away waste. What makes conditions even better is that ocean temperatures change very little in a given spot. They rarely fluctuate more than 1°F (0.5°C) in a day, or 10°F (5.6°C) in a year. That's quite a contrast to the land, where a desert animal may have to survive a chilly 40°F (5°C) night, then a boiling hot 100°F (38°C) day! For these and many other reasons, the ocean is home to a wide variety of life.

HOME SWEET OCEAN

In the ocean, animals and plants can do one of three things. They can float, swim, or settle down. Floating plants and animals, called plankton, generally go with the flow. They are carried along by currents. Animals that actively swim, such as fish, porpoises, sharks, and turtles, are called nekton. These are the ocean's travelers. Animals that settle down are called benthos. These animals include sponges, corals, tube worms, adult mussels, and other creatures that live in and on the shore, coral reefs, or the ocean floor.

These sponges grow on the sea floor off the Florida Keys.

Plant Power   Without tiny plants smaller than the period at the end of this sentence, most ocean creatures would not survive. Phytoplankton—tiny, floating plants, many of which are microscopic—are the basis of ocean life. Minuscule floating animals, called zooplankton, graze on phytoplankton. (These zooplankton are drifters, but they can also move up and down. Many rise to the surface at night to feed, then move as much as 1,311 feet [400 meters] downward to spend the day.) Numerous other animals feed on zooplankton, or on each other. Or they feed on decaying animals and plants and animal droppings. So almost all ocean animals depend on plants, directly or indirectly. The only other food source is bacteria that live in superheated water near hydrothermal vents.

The Ocean Garden   Like a garden, the ocean has places where plants grow well and places where they do not. When the cold waters near the poles are not ice covered, they are rich with phytoplankton. Whales, seals, birds, and fish gather near the Poles during warm seasons to feast on a bounty of food. Yet large stretches of the ocean are almost like desert—where plants do not thrive. In these areas, including much of the Tropics, surface waters are low in nutrients—the chemicals plants need. Often, nutrients are simply locked up in the cold layer of ocean water below. In places called upwellings, cold, nutrient-rich water pushes up from below, causing abundant plant growth that attracts animals. Off the coast of Peru, a tremendous upwelling supports the biggest fishing industry in the world.

• OCEAN POISON: RED TIDE •

In 1987, fourteen whales near Cape Cod died. In North Carolina, some people who had eaten seafood became dizzy and got diarrhea. Swimmers and fishers fell ill. The cause of all these troubles was red tide. A red tide occurs when certain species of phytoplankton grow and reproduce more rapidly than usual. The water becomes thick with the phytoplankton, and sometimes, but not always, appears red.

Certain phytoplankton species naturally release toxins—poisons. During red tides, the toxins in the water increase. Animals that eat these toxins can become sick. The toxins build up in fish and shellfish, which are eaten by people who then become sick and, on some occasions, may die. In recent years, red tides have become more frequent worldwide. Scientists are not sure why. Many countries, such as the United States and Canada, monitor ocean water for red tides. When red tides occur, beaches may be shut down and fishing and shellfishing may be restricted in order to keep people safe.

The Travelers Because ocean food is abundant in some places, and not in others, many animals travel to feed. Some animals also travel to special areas to breed, lay eggs, or give birth. (These areas may be safe from predators or have special conditions the animals need.) Fish, sea turtles, whales, and seabirds migrate long distances for feeding and breeding. Gray whales make a 2,000-mile (3,226-kilometer) round trip from their winter breeding grounds

Female sea turtles lay their eggs and then return to the sea without waiting for the eggs to hatch.

near Mexico to the cold Bering Sea, where food is plentiful in summer.

Female sea turtles spend most of their time at sea. But they climb up onto sandy beaches to lay their eggs. Not just any beach will do. Sea turtles travel as much as 2,000 miles (3,226 kilometers) to return to beaches where they were born. It's amazing that they can find their way, especially considering they may not have been on those beaches for twenty years, since they were hatchlings themselves. Scientists are not sure exactly how the sea turtles find their way. Other migrators, such as birds, navigate using clues such as stars, landmarks, and the earth's magnetic field. Sea turtles may use some of these clues, plus the smell of the water near the beaches where they were born.

OCEAN NEIGHBORHOODS

From the surface, the ocean might seem like one big, unchanging expanse. But really it's not. It has neighborhoods. The neritic province—which extends from low tide to the end of the continental shelf—is relatively shallow, sunlit, and warm. Here seaweed can grow on rocks. For animals, there's lots of food, plus sand to burrow into, rocks to hang on to, and crevices in which to hide. Near islands and shallows close to coasts, coral reefs, kelp forests, and turtle-grass meadows vary the seascape even more. Farther from shore is the oceanic province, or "open ocean." There, organisms choose between the sunlit surface and the dark waters below. Or they may move up or down in the water at certain times of day and night. For a few specially adapted animals, there are even the ultimate ocean "hot spots": hydrothermal vents.

Sunlit Surface The top of the ocean—the sunlit zone—is home to plants, mostly phytoplankton but also seaweeds.

To escape predators, flying fish leap out of the water and glide, using their fins like wings.

Plants cannot live any deeper in the ocean because they need light to carry out photosynthesis. The sunlit zone reaches from 0 to 650 feet (0 to 200 meters) in the clearest waters. But it's only a few feet deep in ocean waters that are clouded by dirt or clogged with plankton.

To stay in this zone, where the sunlight is, phytoplankton are adapted to float. Light frames, spines, and feathery parts spread their body weight out, making them less likely to sink. Seaweeds have balloonlike swellings, filled with air, to keep them afloat. In the sunlit zone live most of the familiar ocean creatures: sea turtles, whales, jellyfish, dolphins, squids, and flying fish.

The Twilight Zone The twilight zone extends from 650 to 3,300 feet (200 to 1,000 meters) deep. Sunlight reaches this zone, but it's not enough for plants to use for photosynthesis. So, here and in the zones below, animals feed on what drops from above—dead animals, dead plants, and animal

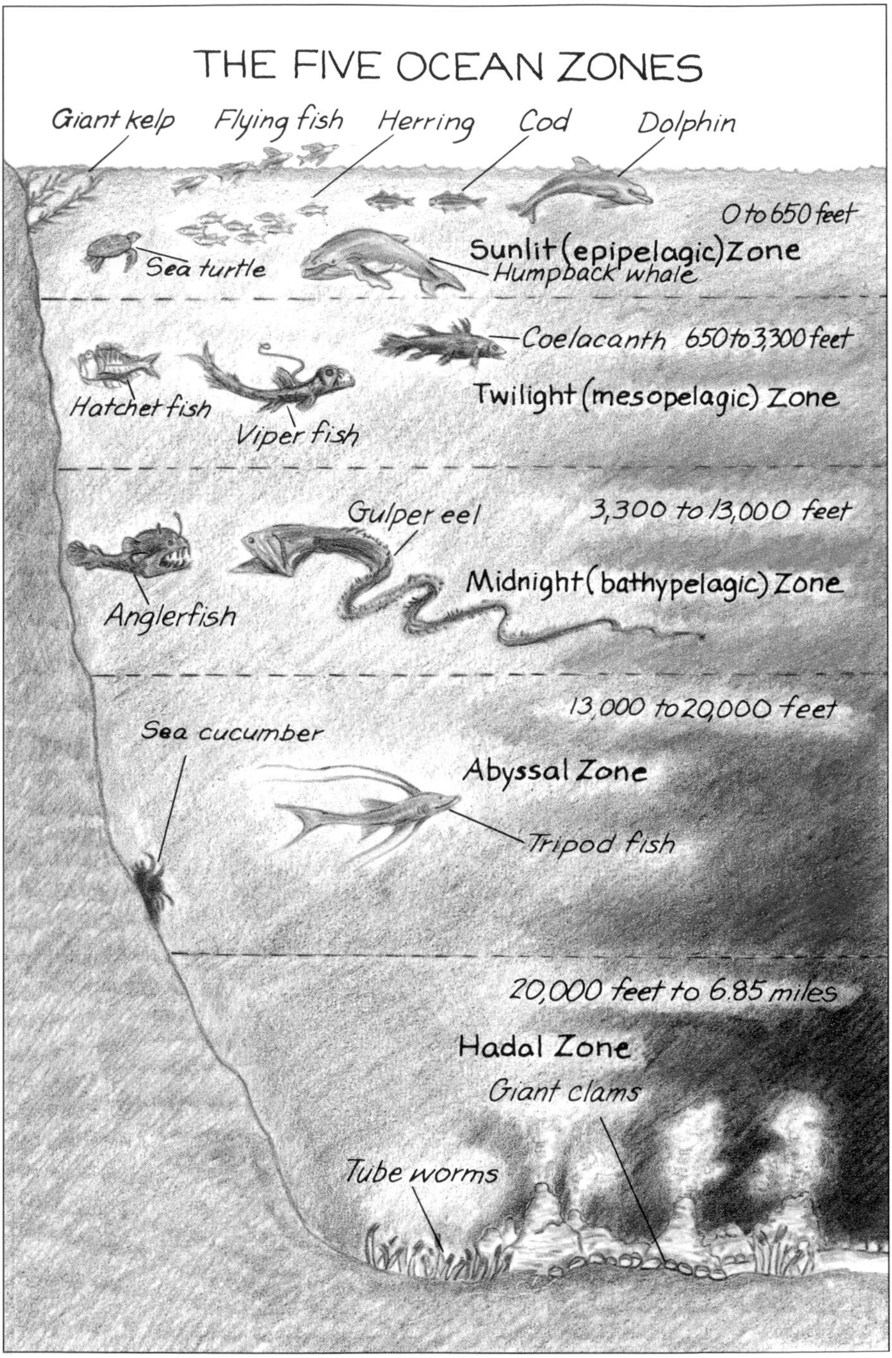

THE FIVE OCEAN ZONES

Giant kelp   Flying fish   Herring   Cod   Dolphin

Sea turtle

Humpback whale

0 to 650 feet

Sunlit (epipelagic) Zone

Coelacanth   650 to 3,300 feet

Twilight (mesopelagic) Zone

Hatchet fish

Viper fish

Gulper eel

3,300 to 13,000 feet

Midnight (bathypelagic) Zone

Anglerfish

Sea cucumber

13,000 to 20,000 feet

Abyssal Zone

Tripod fish

20,000 feet to 6.85 miles

Hadal Zone

Giant clams

Tube worms

· PERPETUAL NIGHT LIGHTS ·

In the twilight and midnight zones, where light is scarce, some creatures make their own light. Bioluminescence—light made by living organisms—serves many different purposes. An anglerfish dangles a lighted lure that grows out of its head. When a fish investigates, the anglerfish gulps it down. Squids sparkle with light, which may help them to recognize one another in the dark. Bioluminescent light can help animals find each other for mating. Comb jellies light up to startle predators, and then escape. Flashlight fish are even trickier. If a predator approaches, a flashlight fish lights up, swims straight, turns off its light, then darts in another direction to escape. Perhaps the strangest use of bioluminescence is for camouflage. Some fish and shrimp in the twilight zone have lighted undersides that mimic the surface light shining far above. Predators looking up are less likely to see these bright shapes than dark shapes swimming overhead!

droppings. Or they feed on one another. This dimly lit zone is home to the coelacanth, a strange, ancient fish, once believed to be extinct but rediscovered in 1938. Other twilight dwellers include 4-inch- (10-centimeter-) long hatchetfish, shaped like hatchets; 3-inch- (7.6-centimeter-) long lantern fish, which are speckled with tiny lights; and many kinds of gelatinous animals, such as midwater jellyfish, as well as creatures called siphonophores and salps. A predator called the viperfish attracts prey with a lighted lure. When an animal moves closer to investigate the light, the viperfish eats it. Overall, like the regions far below, little is known about this zone.

A viperfish has light organs in its mouth and all along its body.

The Midnight Zone   The midnight zone extends from 3,300 to 13,000 feet (1,000 to 4,000 meters) deep. This is the true "deep sea," a cold, lightless world where no plants can survive. Residents include gulper eels, anglerfish, corals, small crustaceans, and gelatinous animals. Overall, food is scarce. Midnight zone animals float or swim slowly, getting meals when and where they can. Perhaps because food is scarce, most deep-sea animals are smaller than those in shallow waters. Animals find food by smell, sound, or vibrations in the water, or by luring it in. Also, in the dark, it can be hard to find a mate. So when a tiny male anglerfish does find a female, he hangs on. He actually attaches himself to the female. The male's body and circulatory system meld with the female's. He never eats again; the female's body completely supports the male's until they die.

How Low Can You Go?   In the ocean's deepest trenches are additional zones. The abyssal zone is from 13,000 to 20,000 feet (4,000 to 6,000 meters) deep. Here scientists have found sea cucumbers—mud-sifting animals that look like squishy cucumbers—and tripodfish, which prop themselves up on long, stiff fins. Still deeper is the hadal zone, which reaches from 20,000 feet (6,000 meters) to the ocean's deepest known point, 6.85 miles (11 kilometers) deep. Animals survive even here. Scientists found a flounderlike fish at 6.8 miles (10 kilometers) deep! How these animals survive at such high pressure—1,000 times greater than the air pressure in which we live—is still not well understood.

Hot Spots of Life   Deep in the ocean is a strange bacterium. Like a plant, it can make its own food. But it doesn't use sunlight for energy. Instead, it gets energy from the chemical bonds in hydrogen sulfide—a chemical deadly to most animals. This energy-extracting process is called chemosynthesis. The chemosynthetic bacteria live in communities of animals near hydrothermal vents, discovered in 1977. At these vents, plumes of hot, sulfur-rich water spurt up from the ocean floor. Heated by flowing through volcanic rocks, the water is superhot—more than 750°F (399°C)! Chemosynthetic bacteria live in the tissues of red-

Scientists were amazed to find giant tube worms, clams, and crabs living in superheated water near hydrothermal vents.

· INTO THE UNKNOWN ·

For most of human history, people have learned about what was in the ocean by examining what was pulled up in fishing nets. But nets miss a whole host of ocean animals, such as deep-ocean creatures and tiny animals that slip through holes in the nets. (Jellyfish and comb jellies are shredded by nets and become unrecognizable goo!) Today, scientists can bypass nets and observe ocean animals in their environment. By scuba diving, scientists can reach the top few hundred feet of the ocean. In pressurized diving suits, they can reach 1,440 feet (439 meters) deep. Going deeper requires an underwater vehicle—a submersible. In 1960, two men in the submersible *Trieste* made it all the way to the ocean's deepest spot, the Mariana Trench. Soon after, another crew visited it in the *Archimede*. Since then, only one other submersible, Japan's *Kaiko*—which contained only video cameras, not people—has even tried to go as deep.

The deepest part of the ocean is almost 7 miles (11 kilometers) down, which isn't far to travel on land. But in the ocean, the farther down you go, the higher the water pressure. At the bottom, the pressure is 16,000 pounds per square inch (1,125

tipped tube worms and clams that cluster near the vents. Spider crabs and odd, tentacled animals also live near these vents, which may form chimneylike piles of sediment as tall as a fifteen-story building. When the hot, mineral-rich water in the vents hits the cold ocean water, the minerals precipitate out, forming the rock "chimneys."

MYSTERIES OF THE DEEP

Every year, scientists search for the elusive giant squid. So far, they've only found small specimens, and large tenta-

kilograms per square centimeter). That's like having the weight of an entire school bus pressing on your big toe! An underwater vehicle must be strong to withstand such pressure. In the past, underwater vehicles were heavy, bulky, awkward, and expensive.

Recently, engineers have been experimenting with lightweight metals and ceramics to create submersibles that are more maneuverable and less expensive. One submersible, called *Deep Flight*, looks like a chunky underwater airplane. It carries one person, who lies in a harness like a hang glider pilot. *Deep Flight* is designed to race, roll, and maneuver like a dolphin. But it can only descend a few thousand feet. Already designed, but unbuilt, is *Deep Flight II*, which could reach all the way to the ocean bottom.

Some scientists favor putting money into building unmanned vehicles instead of those like *Deep Flight II*. Unmanned vehicles, which are even less expensive than the new submersibles, could take photos and transmit them to boats on the surface. Still, the deep lures explorers who believe that people can learn more about the ocean floor by seeing it firsthand.

cles. By the size of these tentacles, scientists estimate the squid can be as long as 65 feet (20 meters). But no one has ever seen a whole giant squid alive.

Whether the giant squid exists is only one of the many questions facing oceanographers. Another puzzle is why deep-sea creatures are so diverse—so varied in species and form. After all, there aren't many creatures in the deepest parts of the ocean. And there's not much food to eat down there. Yet the animals that are there vary tremendously in form. No one knows why. Scientists would like to find out.

You might think that by now scientists would know all the creatures that live in the ocean. But a few years ago, a film crew working in the ocean near Baja, California, stumbled upon something immense. It was a new kind of jellyfish, almost 20 feet (6 meters) long! The top, or "bell," of the bright purple jellyfish was almost 3 feet (0.9 meter) wide. Hundreds of these jellyfish swam by the startled crew, who recorded the event on film. This jellyfish, previously unknown to science, is just one of the many oceanic discoveries of recent years. The ocean is teeming with strange, little-known creatures, adapted to ocean life in remarkable ways.

BREATHING, STAYING WARM, AND SWIMMING

Imagine being able to hold your breath for two hours. Elephant seals can. This breath-holding ability helps ocean animals such as whales, seals, sea turtles, and penguins, who dive deeply but need to breathe air. These animals also make each breath count. Whales can exchange 80 to 90 percent of the air in their lungs for new air when they take a breath. Humans, by contrast, can only exchange about 25 percent per breath. Penguins and marine mammals—dolphins, seals, and whales—also store unusually large

When seals like this harbor seal dive, oxygen stored in their muscles helps them to stay underwater for long periods of time.

amounts of oxygen in their muscles and blood. They can use this oxygen when they're diving so that they won't need air for a while. In really long dives, some diving animals cut off blood circulation to less important body parts until they can resurface to breathe.

The Goods on Gills   Fish don't need to breathe air. Their gills extract oxygen from water. Most fish use muscles to pump water over their gills. But a tuna just opens its mouth and swims hard. Water flows into its mouth, over its gills, and out its gill slits. That saves the work of pumping water with muscles. However, if the tuna stops swimming, it suffocates.

Fat, Fur, and Antifreeze   Cold water can cool an animal's body fifty to one hundred times faster than cool air. That's why air at 70°F (21°C) might feel just fine to you, but swimming in a pool filled with water at that temperature can make you feel cold. In the ocean, which can be as cold as 28°F (-2.2°C), animals must cope with the extreme cold. Near Antarctica, fish called notothenioids make their own natural antifreeze. This antifreeze prevents ice crystals in the blood and cells from growing large enough to damage the fish's cells and internal organs. Reportedly, the antifreeze is three hundred times more effective than the antifreeze people buy for their cars!

Marine mammals, which are warm-blooded, must keep their internal body temperature high. So, many are insulated. Between their skin and their muscles, whales have a layer of fat called blubber. It can be 20 inches (51 centimeters) thick! Blubber can keep a seal's inner body temperature around 100°F (38°C) while it swims in water that is close to freezing. Instead of blubber, sea otters rely on fur to keep them warm. Their fur is the thickest in the animal world.

Swimming Styles   Ocean animals swim by different methods. Scallops spend most of their time resting on the ocean bottom. But when they do swim, they flap their shells open, then pull them closed. This squeezes out water, pushing them in a zigzagging path, using a kind of "jet propulsion." Squid also travel this way, squeezing water out of tiny siphons to push their bodies along. Eels, worms, and sea snakes move in an S pattern. Their bodies bend, pushing from side to side and propelling them forward at the same time. A fish's tail works in a similar way, pressing first to one side, then to the other. Whales' tails, which are horizontal, move up and down instead. Fish and many other ocean animals—penguins and dolphins for instance—are also torpedo shaped. Their streamlined, compact forms slide easily through the water, so they use less energy to swim.

In order to move, squid use jets of water squirted out of their bodies.

Sink or Float?   To swim near the surface, a fish must accomplish two things. It must move forward. And it must avoid sinking. To help stay afloat, many fish have swim bladders—special bags of gases such as oxygen and nitrogen—inside their bodies. They add or withdraw gas from the swim bladder to control their buoyancy—how high they float in the water. (For the same reason, scuba divers add or release air from air-filled vests.) Sharks, which don't have swim bladders, must constantly swim in order not to sink. (But some sharks do rest by basking on the ocean floor.)

BRUSH UP ON BUOYANCY

Learn more about buoyancy by exploring it firsthand.

Here are the materials you will need:
- Four sealable plastic (Ziploc) bags, medium to small
- A straw
- A bucket, bowl, or sink full of water
- A faucet where you can get more water

1. Your first bag should be empty of air. If it's not, unseal it, flatten it with your hands to get the air out, then seal it.

2. Fill a second bag entirely full of air. (Blow air into it, using a straw if you wish.) Seal the bag.

3. Fill a third bag entirely full of water. Seal it.

4. Fill a fourth bag half full of water. Insert a straw into the air-filled half of the bag. Close the seal around the straw. Blow more air into the bag until it's plump with air. (Be careful not to suck in water in the process!) Remove the straw and seal the bag.

5. Place the bags in the bucket, bowl, or sink of water. Observe the results. Which bag floated the highest? The lowest?

6. Add more water to the half air/half water bag. How does that change how high it floats in the water?

Think about how the results of these activities relate to the way a jellyfish floats, or the way a fish's swim bladder operates.

Note: Water's buoyancy—its tendency to support the weight of objects in it—has to do with density. An object less dense than water will float on water. An object denser than water will sink in water. An object of an intermediate density will sink partway down and then float there, underwater.

No Bones About It   On land, an animal the size of a whale shark would need tremendous, heavy bones to support its weight. But these 44-ton (40-metric-ton) animals can survive in water. Yet they don't have a bone in their bodies! Instead, a shark's skeleton is made of cartilage—a soft bonelike material. Animals whose skeletons are made mostly of cartilage are called elasmobranchs. Skates, rays, and sharks belong to this group. (You have cartilage, too, in the tip of your nose. To find it, run your finger down the ridge of your

· THAT SINKING FEELING ·

When you float and swim in a pool, you feel lighter than you do on land. That's because of water's buoyancy. It supports your body as you move. This same buoyancy, which is even stronger in salt water, makes it possible for many ocean creatures to survive. A comb jelly, for instance, is a shapeless blob on land. But in the ocean, it's a delicate, translucent animal. Water's buoyancy also supports tiny floating plankton, limp seaweeds, and even the humongous weight of whales. Without the support of ocean water, a blue whale would suffocate under its own weight!

nose. Where the hard bone ends, the firm but flexible cartilage begins.)

FEEDING AND DEFENSE

Finding a meal and not becoming a meal are two major challenges all animals face. The ways marine animals meet these needs range from the familiar to the utterly bizarre.

Filtering Food In the ocean, many animals filter feed, meaning they filter food particles and small organisms out of the water. Clams pull water in through their snorkel-like siphons and strain food tidbits out. Tiny hairs sweep water through the holes in living sponges so that they can strain particles of food out. Corals, sea cucumbers, barnacles, and worms trap food from the water passing by, using sticky tentacles, strings of mucus, nets, and feathery legs. Gray whales filter feed on a giant scale. They gulp mud and water and filter it through a comblike material called baleen.

Amphipods are an important part of the ocean food chain. These amphipods, called scuds, have been photographed through a microscope.

The baleen sifts small crustaceans called amphipods from water and mud by the ton.

Fast Foods and Shocking Behavior Whales are divided into two main groups, according to how they feed. Baleen whales are the filter feeders. Toothed whales such as orcas hunt larger prey. Orcas, or killer whales, work in groups to round up prey such as seals. Other marine predators have their own adaptations. Octopuses have long arms with suckers to catch prey. Sharks have several rows of very sharp teeth. As one row of teeth wears out, the next row takes its place. For shock value, electric rays probably win the prize. They can produce 220 volts of electricity, stunning fish for easy capture.

A Strong Defense For a prey animal, the best defense is to stay away from predators. Scallops can smell a starfish approaching and will often quickly swim away. Feather duster worms pull in their feathery tentacles when large animals approach. Clams close their shells. Squids squeeze out clouds of ink to hide themselves as they flee. For ani-

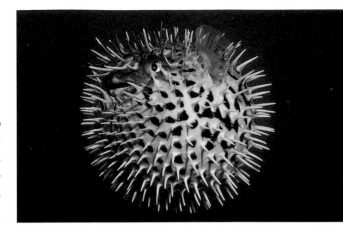

A spiny puffer fish inflates itself, becoming too big and prickly for most predators to eat.

mals that don't flee, other tricks work. Cowries shoot acid at their attackers. Puffer fish puff up, spines sticking out. This makes them look, if not intimidating, at least difficult to eat! Starfish will abandon an arm and crabs will break off their own claws, all in order to escape. (The arms and claws grow back.)

Ocean Hide and Seek   First looks can be deceptive in the ocean realm. What looks like seaweed may be a sea dragon—a relative of the sea horse. A slender black spike could be a sea urchin spine, or a shrimpfish instead. Shrimpfish hide, nose down, among sea urchin spines, where their slender, black-striped bodies blend in. These natural disguises help prey animals to hide. Cuttlefish, sea horses, and flounders camouflage themselves—blending in with the background. They can change their skin colors and patterns to match the seaweed, rocks, or sand they are near. Many marine animals, including dolphins, fish, and penguins, are dark on top and light on the bottom. This pattern, called countershading, helps them hide. When seen from above, their dark top matches the darkness of the ocean

• SAVE THE . . . *SHARKS?* •

With rows of sharp teeth, and a powerful bite, sharks don't seem like creatures that need protection. But hundreds of thousands of sharks are being killed annually. Worldwide, shark populations are plummeting.

The reason sharks are declining is overfishing. As other ocean fish populations decrease, people are switching to eating shark steak. And sharks are being caught to make shark fin soup—an Asian delicacy. In a day, a single ship may catch hundreds of sharks, cut off their fins, and dump the dying creatures back into the ocean. Sharks are also killed for their cartilage, which some people believe helps cure disease. (These claims are scientifically unproven.) Other sharks are caught accidentally, in nets used to catch squid and other fish.

The world's four hundred shark species vary from the whale shark, which eats only tiny plankton, to the great white shark, which eats seals, to the tiny cookie cutter shark, which takes little bites out of whales. Sharks have good eyesight—seven times better than humans—and an incredible sense of smell. On the shark's head are electoreceptors called the *ampullae of Lorenzini*, which can sense the earth's magnetic field. This organ also senses subtle electric fields that surround other animals. Despite their amazing senses and immune system, sharks are particu-

depths. Yet their light underside, when seen from below, blends with the bright sunlit surface.

FAMILIES, FRIENDS, AND RELATIONS

Like tadpoles that become frogs, many marine animals look and behave differently at different stages in their lives. For part of the time, jellyfish are medusae—the floating jelly-

larly vulnerable to extinction because of their life cycle. Most grow slowly, some taking fifteen or more years to mature before they can reproduce. Females of some shark species give birth to only two young at a time.

It is unknown how the loss of sharks will affect the ocean ecosystem. Like wolves, sharks are top predators and help control the numbers of some prey. Near Tasmania, an island off Australia, sharks were killed in huge numbers. As a result, octopuses—the sharks' main prey—increased drastically. These octopuses gobbled up many more spiny lobsters, devastating the local spiny lobster harvest.

What about the danger of sharks to people? You're more likely to be killed by lightning or a bee sting. Still, that's not particularly comforting to the fifty to seventy-five people who are attacked by sharks each year worldwide. Five to ten people die from such attacks, mostly attacks by great white sharks, bullhead sharks, and tiger sharks. Most other sharks are harmless.

Overall, sharks are in more danger from people than people are from sharks. Scientists hope action will soon be taken to save the world's sharks. In April 1993, the United States passed regulations limiting the number of sharks that can be killed off its shores. This was a good first step. But scientists and conservationists are concerned that the number of sharks that can legally be killed is still much too high.

fish we know best. But they also spend time as polyps on the ocean floor. Polyps look like tiny, tentacled anemones—more like flowers than animals. Eventually they form stacks of tiny medusae, which break off, turn over, and float away. These medusae grow larger, becoming the saucer-shaped jellyfish we recognize. Young lobsters, crabs, barnacles, and sea urchins also change greatly during their lives.

· JELLYFISH AND THEIR KIN ·

Stretch out your arms as wide as you can. Now imagine a jelly-fish even wider than that. The lion's mane jellyfish, one of the world's biggest jellyfish, can be 8 feet (2.4 meters) in diameter and 2 feet (61 centimeters) high! Most jellyfish are smaller. Pink, blue, yellow, milky, or even striped, jellyfish vary in both color and shape. Some look like Frisbees, while others are more rounded, like squishy soccer balls that float. All of them move by a kind of jet propulsion, squeezing their bodies to push water out below their dome-shaped bells. But their swimming is weak and doesn't get them very far. Usually, they end up wherever the currents carry them.

Lion's mane jellyfish   Portuguese man-of-war

They hatch from eggs to become tiny floating larvae that look almost nothing like their adult forms. Although these larvae can control their movements somewhat, they generally just drift wherever currents take them. These larvae are part of the plankton, the mass of animals and plants that float through the ocean realm.

A jellyfish's sting is caused by tiny cells called nematocysts. These cells cover its entire body, although they are concentrated in its tentacles. When an animal touches a jellyfish, a stinging cell shoots out a barbed thread that sticks in the animal's skin. The barbs release venom—a poison—that paralyzes small prey such as shrimp, fish, and plankton. Then it's dinnertime: with its tentacles and fleshy folds, the jellyfish pulls its prey into its mouth.

Jellyfish may look like jelly. But they definitely aren't fish. These boneless creatures belong to a group of animals called the Cnidaria, which includes comb jellies, anemones, corals, and the famous Portuguese man-of-wars. Many of these animals have stinging cells to catch prey, as jellyfish do. All have simple, primitive bodies—like bags with only one opening: a mouth. Hidden underneath a jellyfish's dome-shaped bell, the mouth gathers in food and also spits waste out.

A Portuguese man-of-war may look like one animal. But it's actually many animals living together. Each animal plays a special role in the colony. One forms the gigantic, gas-filled bag that acts as a float and sail. Other animals join to form deadly lacy tentacles that dangle down. These tentacles, covered with stinging cells, may reach 50 feet (15 meters) in length.

Social Lives   Marine animals have "family" lives as variable as the ocean is large. Female sea turtles crawl up on beaches and lay their eggs in the sand. The young turtles hatch, dig out of the sand, and make their way to the ocean all alone, without parents around. In contrast, whales live in family groups, communicating by complex songs that can

A male sea horse gives birth to live young, after carrying the female's eggs in his pouch.

be heard as far as 500 miles (806 kilometers) away. Dolphins touch fins and snap their jaws to "talk" with the other members of their pod—a dolphin group. Fish swim in schools, their movements perfectly synchronized as they swim. Sea horse males, not the females, become pregnant. (The female deposits the eggs in the male's specially made pouch.) Even stranger still, many fish species change sex during their lives. Some turn from males into females and some do the reverse.

ANIMAL DIVERSITY

From sea horses to scallops to seals, the ocean supports a high diversity or variety of animal life. Scientists divide the world's animal species into thirty-three groups called phyla. One phylum lives only on land. Sixteen phyla are found only in the ocean. Sixteen phyla contain animals found on land *and* animals found in the ocean. What this means is that the ocean, with a total of 32 phyla, contains the greatest variety of animal body shapes and functions of any place on earth. Just think about the tremendous difference between a comb jelly, a peanut worm, and a whale!

❦ 6 ❧
PEOPLE AND OCEANS

At the southern tip of the islands that make up Japan is a coral bump barely visible at high tide. Ten feet (about 3 meters) by 16 feet (about 5 meters) wide, it seems insignificant. Yet Japan spent $300 million to protect it with concrete and steel walls. Why? Because it gives Japan the fishing, mining, and oil drilling rights to 154,440 square miles (400,000 square kilometers) of surrounding ocean. And the Japanese, like people all over the world, are scrambling for the right to gather ocean riches.

THE RACE TO CATCH THE BIG FISH

Chief among the ocean's riches are its fish, crabs, squid, whales, and other living creatures. For thousands of years, people have harvested these animals for food, clothing, and other needs. But today the fishing lifestyle is in danger in much of the world because the populations of many ocean creatures are plummeting.

Watching the Numbers The decline is most noticeable among the ocean species people eat. The number of bluefin tuna caught in the western Atlantic has decreased by about 80 percent since 1970. In coastal waters off the United States, Atlantic salmon, California halibut, mackerel, cod, flounder, haddock, swordfish, Pacific Ocean perch, and shad are all declining, according to the National Fish and Wildlife Foundation. The main reason for the decline, scientists say, is that people are overfishing—catching too many fish. (Pollution also plays a role, as will be discussed later on.) Worldwide, the catch of many other edible ocean species, such as lobsters and clams, is declining as well.

To fully recover from overfishing, some fish populations might need decades with drastically reduced fishing. But who will be allowed to continue fishing and who will not? Will fishers be allowed to catch enough to make a profit? The questions remain. As consumer favorites such as cod, salmon, haddock, and tuna decline, the fishing industry has turned to catching mackerel, squid, orange roughie, and even Antarctic krill.

Tangled Web   The overfishing problem is not quite as simple as too many people catching too many fish. It's a tangle of troubles and complex problems. Just consider these fishing issues:

- Worldwide, millions of people feed their families by fishing in small boats and canoes, with small nets. For others, fishing is big business, carried out by factory fishing boats—huge boats where fish can be cleaned, processed, and canned right on board. These boats may cost as much as $48 million apiece. In some countries, these big boats and little boats compete for the same fish. Many small-scale fishers are having to buy expensive equipment and work harder than ever to compete with others trying to harvest the dwindling numbers of fish.
- Trawling—fishing by dragging weighted nets along the ocean bottom—is a widespread technique. Unfortunately,

trawling can destroy reefs, sponge populations, and other ocean-bottom communities.

- In the open ocean, fishers set up nets, some as much as 40 miles (65 kilometers) wide. These nets scoop up and kill practically every creature in their path.
- During the 1970s and 1980s, people spent billions of dollars to buy and build boats to make money off large-scale fishing. But now the numbers of fish are decreasing, and the boats are losing money as they harvest the few fish that remain. Yet governments continue helping out the fishing industry with billions of dollars in investments, loans, and tax breaks that encourage them to expand.
- Millions of tons of fish and other sea creatures are simply thrown away. This is bycatch—the fish, dolphins, sharks, threatened and endangered sea turtles, and other animals that are caught in the nets, hauled up on deck, but then discarded, usually dead. For every pound (.45 kilograms) of shrimp caught in the Gulf of Mexico, 4.2 pounds (1.9 kilograms) of fish bycatch are thrown away.
- About one-third of the world's fish harvest is not eaten by people. Most of that third goes to feed pets and livestock

• TURTLE TROUBLES •

In the 1990s, the United States took action to reduce one kind of bycatch—sea turtles. Of the seven species of sea turtles, five are endangered or threatened. The U.S. government enacted regulations to require many shrimpers to install turtle excluder devices (TEDs) on their nets. These devices help sea turtles to escape from shrimpers' nets. Their use by shrimpers on the Atlantic coast of the United States has decreased the killing of turtles. But some Gulf coast shrimpers have rebelled against the use of TEDs. Many have sewn their nets closed, destroyed the TEDs, and even killed sea turtles on purpose to show their anger about TED regulations. Even though TEDs have been shown to decrease bycatch and improve shrimping efficiency, some Gulf coast shrimpers remain unconvinced.

such as chickens. In Chile, many poor people have a difficult time getting fish to eat because so many fish are sold to richer countries for use as pet food and livestock feed.

• Lately, the world's oceans have seemed like the wild, wild west. Big fishing boats from many nations are traveling far from their own shores, searching for fish. Sometimes these boats sneak into other countries' waters in order to illegally catch fish. So far, enforcing fishing laws has proved difficult.

Issues such as these are making fishing worldwide ever more challenging. It's tough on the ocean ecosystem. And it's tough on many people who not only care about the ocean but also depend on it for their livelihood.

Fish Farming: The Possibilities   If the ocean doesn't produce enough fish, why not raise them in captivity? Aquaculture—the raising of domestic fish, shrimp, and other aquatic creatures—does work in some cases, especially for freshwater fish. Unfortunately, mariculture—aquaculture of ocean fish—is more difficult and can be environmentally damaging. Fish are raised in underwater pens in coastal waters. Trouble is, the fish are vulnerable to coastal pollution. Disease spreads quickly because the fish are crowded close together in the pens. And the fish produce so many droppings that they pollute the water in which they live. In Honduras, Mexico, and many tropical countries, tremendous areas of coastal mangrove swamp have been destroyed to make ponds to raise shrimp. All in all, mariculture is unlikely to meet the world's increasing need for food.

Some oysters are raised on oyster farms off the coast of Washington State.

· WHO OWNS THE OCEAN? ·

Until the twentieth century, the ocean was largely a "no-man's-land." Countries only controlled waters within a few miles of their shores. But after World War II, countries began claiming larger and larger sections of the ocean for themselves. The United Nations stepped in to try to resolve the conflicts that arose. It took decades of negotiations to do the job. But finally, in 1994, the United Nations' Law of the Sea Treaty was ratified.

The Law of the Sea Treaty states that nations can claim and defend 12 nautical miles (22.2 kilometers) of territory extending from their coasts. Countries also have the right to an Exclusive Economic Zone that extends 200 nautical miles (370 kilometers) from their shores. In this zone, they can explore, use, and man-

Solving the Problem The solution to the overfishing problem is a difficult one. Human population is growing rapidly. Demand for food is high. Managing the ocean's fish without depleting them will require cooperation among many countries. Changes in the fishing industry will affect millions of people's livelihoods. Success is possible, however. In the Philippines, some local communities have been given control over fishing grounds. They are restoring mangrove swamps, regulating fishing, and successfully managing their catches. These small-scale projects give hope that fishing can be sensibly managed elsewhere in the world.

MORE OCEAN RICHES

When some people look at the ocean, they see a home for fish and whales. But others see energy. Crashing waves and rising tides may one day be harnessed to create large

age all natural resources. This allows oil drilling, fishing, and other activities. (The treaty also allows countries to control resources found on the continental shelf, even if it extends beyond 200 nautical miles [370 kilometers].) All the rest of the ocean and the resources it contains are considered international territory with boundaries set by treaties or customs that give all countries similar rights and duties. All countries will share the benefits from these ocean resources.

There are still a few "bugs" to work out in the Law of the Sea Treaty. The borders of some overlapping territories are still being resolved. The United States has signed the treaty but has not ratified it, meaning the Senate has not yet approved the treaty. But the United States and other countries are honoring and abiding by the treaty, in general.

amounts of electricity. In the meantime, oil, natural gas, and coal are harvested from beneath the ocean floor.

Digging Deep   In the last few decades, much of the international race to control the ocean has been fueled by the desire to mine the ocean floor. Already oil and natural gas are pumped from the ocean floor. So far, no one has tried deep ocean mining; it would be difficult, expensive, and possibly environmentally damaging. But polymetallic nodules, which are lumps of mixed minerals, lie deep in the ocean. The valuable minerals they contain—iron, copper, manganese, nickel, and cobalt—may one day be mined.

Catch a Wave   Scientists are working on devices to harness wave energy and tidal energy. These devices use waves or tides to push floats up and down, or to push water and/or air back and forth inside a tank. This energy is harnessed to turn a turbine, which can then generate electricity. Tidal-powered devices have been generating electricity in several locations in Europe for over twenty-five years. But so far the technology is expensive and practical only in limited areas. Another promising technology uses the temperature difference between warm surface water and cold deep water to generate electricity.

OTHER ENVIRONMENTAL ISSUES

Sick seals. Dying dolphins. Fish with cancer. Turtles with tumors. Ocean animals have been showing alarming signs of trouble recently. In 1988, 25,000 harbor seals died in the North and Baltic Seas. In the late 1980s, hundreds of dead dolphins and dead seals showed up on the Atlantic coast of the United States. At first, scientists suspected pollution had killed the seals and dolphins. But it turned out the di-

modern society. Even if you never eat a shrimp or ocean fish, they may show up in your life. Chitosan, made from the shells of shrimp and crabs, is used by doctors to stitch people's wounds. The blood of horseshoe crabs is used in laboratories to test for contaminants in pharmaceutical drugs during manufacturing. (The crabs, after some blood is extracted, are returned to the ocean alive.) Scientists all over the world are investigating new uses for chemicals found in ocean creatures. Coral is being considered as a bone substitute for patients who need human bone replaced. Anticancer substances in corals, virus-fighting chemicals in sea squirts, and heart-disease fighting chemicals in sea sponges are all being studied. The more scientists know about the ocean, the more remarkable a resource it seems to be.

rect cause of death was disease. However, the animals' bodies *did* contain very high concentrations of pollutants such as polychlorinated biphenyls (PCBs), toxins produced by industry. Further studies by scientists showed that seals who eat fish from polluted waters are less able to fight off disease. So the seal die-off and the dolphin problem could be related to pollution, after all. In this instance, as in others, the effects of pollution, overfishing, and many other ocean problems can be interrelated.

Pollution Problems Like land biomes, the ocean biome is plagued by pollution. Oil leaks into the ocean from boat motors, offshore oil drilling rigs, and oil tankers that wreck at sea. Nuclear waste, toxic waste, and garbage are sometimes deliberately dumped into the sea. Industries release harmful chemicals into harbors, bays, and the ocean.

Ocean pollution also comes from the land. Polluted

rivers dump their polluted loads into the sea. Rain washes lawn fertilizers, pesticides, discarded oil, gas spilled at gas stations, soap, paint, and other pollutants into the ocean. Coastal towns and cities that cannot handle their sewage dump it into the ocean. Even if water passes through a treatment plant, it may not be cleansed well enough to remove all the complex chemicals people and industries dump down their drains.

Plastic in the Ocean   These days if you're beachcombing, you're as likely to find plastic and garbage as seashells. Even remote Pacific islands are strewn with plastic bags, six-pack rings, detergent bottles, old fishing nets, and fishing lines. This trash comes both from land and ocean. People on ships pitch their garbage overboard. Garbage from land is also dumped out at sea. Plastic trash is particularly hazardous to ocean animals because it is long-lasting. Sea turtles eat plastic bags, mistaking them for one of their favorite foods: jellyfish. Plastic garbage kills whales, dolphins, seals, and birds by choking them or blocking their digestive tracts. Discarded fishing nets float through the ocean for years, entangling and killing seabirds, dolphins, turtles, fish, and more.

Habitat Destruction   The destruction of ocean habitat occurs in many different ways. The French government recently blew up a Pacific coral reef in order to test its nuclear weapons. Fishing boats trawl, scraping the ocean bottom, destroying fragile corals and sponges. Oil drilling, mining, and coal excavation destroy habitat, too. And coastal development can destroy wetlands, which are nursery grounds for young ocean creatures such as fish, shrimp, and crabs.

Entangled in a six-pack ring, this gull will not survive for long.

Ozone No Zone   The ozone layer—a layer of gas high above the earth—shields the earth from damaging solar radiation. But lately, the earth's ozone has been thinning because of air pollution. Scientists are concerned that the extra radiation hitting the earth could harm ocean animals and plants.

The Global Climate   These days, the earth's climate is warming. Scientists believe this may be in part because of air pollutants released by automobiles, industry, backyard grills, lawn mowers, and the burning of tropical forests. Even a slight warming of the ocean could impact many animals, who are adapted to constant conditions. Animals on coasts and on coral reefs could be particularly affected. As the earth's climate warms, sea levels also rise. Currently, sea levels along 90 percent of the earth's shorelines are rising.

WHAT'S BEING DONE TO CONSERVE OCEANS

In 1992, representatives from countries all over the world met to talk about ocean problems. They strengthened laws to help prevent the dumping of garbage, toxic waste, plastic, and other pollutants in coastal waters. This convention, the International Convention for the Prevention of Pollution from Ships, also called MARPOL, is just one of the many efforts being made to conserve oceans. Here are a few other positive actions being taken to help ocean habitats and animals:

• In Costa Rica, Boy Scout troops are helping clear beaches of debris and keeping track of sea turtle nests. Their presence also seems to help keep egg poachers—people who would steal the eggs—away.

• Near Mexico's Yucatán peninsula is the Sian Ka'an Biosphere Reserve. In this reserve, local people are given leases to catch lobsters in certain waters. To protect their jobs, they've become local guardians, keeping the waters clean, protecting the habitat, and maintaining the lobster population by not harvesting female lobsters carrying eggs.

• In the early 1990s, the United Nations passed several resolutions calling for countries to stop using large, high-seas drift nets—the ones that can be as much as 40 miles (65 kilometers) wide. Not all countries are complying with the measure, but the resolution is a step in the right direction.

The efforts mentioned here are only a tiny sampling of the work being done to help conserve oceans. Diplomats, environmental activists, people who fish, local farmers, movie stars, kids, mothers, fathers, grandparents—all kinds of

*Everyone can help
to keep beaches
clean and beautiful!*

people—are pitching in to help oceans. On the shores of many countries, people are cleaning beaches, saving sea turtles, replanting mangrove swamps, reducing pollution, and working for better laws to protect the ocean. These people care about ocean animals and habitats and know that everyone's future depends on the ocean's health. To find out how you can join in ocean-saving efforts, read the next section.

RESOURCES AND WHAT
YOU CAN DO TO HELP

Here's what you can do to help ensure that oceans are conserved:

• Learn more by reading books and watching videos and television programs about the ocean. Check your local library, bookstore, and video store for resources. Here are just a few of the materials available for further reading:

Deep Sea Vents by John F. Waters (Cobblehill, 1994).
"Diminishing Returns: Exploiting the Ocean's Bounty" by Michael Parfit, *National Geographic* (November 1995).
Global Marine Biological Diversity edited by Elliott A. Norse (Island Press, 1993).
How to Be an Ocean Scientist in Your Own Home by Seymour Simon (J.B. Lippincott, 1988).
The Oceans: A Book of Questions and Answers by Don Groves (John Wiley and Sons, 1989).
Oceans: The Illustrated Library of the Earth edited by Robert E. Stevenson, Ph.D., and Frank H. Talbot, Ph.D. (Rodale Press, 1993).
Pioneering Ocean Depths by Sandra Markle (Atheneum, 1995).
The Random House Atlas of the Oceans edited by Dr. Danny Elder and Dr. John Penetta (Random House, 1991).

Safari Beneath the Sea by Diane Swanson (Whitecap Books, 1994).

The Strange World of Deep-Sea Vents by R.V. Foder (Enslow, 1991).

Whales, Dolphins, and Porpoises by Mark Carwardine (Dorling Kindersley, 1995).

• For more information on conservation issues related to the ocean, contact the following organizations:

American Cetacean Society
P.O. Box 2639
San Pedro, CA 90731-0943
Phone 1-310-548-6279
(Their focus is whales
and dolphins.)

Caribbean Conservation Corporation
P.O. Box 2866
Gainesville, FL 32602
Phone 1-904-373-6441
(Their focus is sea turtles.)

American Oceans Campaign
725 Arizona Avenue,
Ste. 102
Santa Monica, CA 90401
Phone 1-310-576-6162

Center for Marine Conservation
1725 DeSales Street, NW
Washington, DC 20036
Phone 1-202-429-5609
(They cover all ocean issues, especially plastic pollution. They help manage coastal cleanups worldwide.)

If you like the job these organizations are doing, consider becoming a member.

• To explore oceans through your computer, contact the following companies and organizations:

Ingram

Phone 1-800-937-8000

(They sell *Microsoft Oceans,* an interactive CD-ROM. Your local computer store may also sell copies.)

Journey North Project

125 North First Street

Minneapolis, MN 55402

Phone 1-612-339-6959

e-mail jnorth@learner.org

(The Journey North Project links scientists with students through the Internet. Weekly reports of whale sightings keep students up to date on the progress of humpback whales migrating in the Atlantic Ocean.)

Monterey Bay Aquarium Online

(They have a worldwide web site you can access at: http://www.mbayaq.org/)

National Oceanic and Atmospheric Administration

National Marine Sanctuaries

(They have worldwide web pages you can browse to learn about ocean issues. To access their web pages, contact: http://www.nos.noaa.gov/ocrm)

- Improve ocean habitat by participating in coastal cleanups each fall. For information on beach cleanups in your area, contact the Center for Marine Conservation at the address and phone number above. Or organize your own beach cleanup, any day of the year!

- Work to reduce your use of plastics that may end up in the marine environment. Plastic bags, ropes, bottles, and other items can kill wildlife. When you go to a store, bring cloth bags, old paper bags, or old plastic bags. Use these bags instead of getting new bags each trip. When you purchase an item, decide whether you really need a bag to carry it. Politely tell the checkout person if you don't need one. (Always carry the receipt for the item with you in case you need to prove you paid for it.) For cloth bags and other environmental products, contact the following company for a catalog:

Seventh Generation
Colchester, Vermont 05446-1672
Phone 1-800-456-1177

- Work with your family to reduce your use of toxic chemicals that can pollute coastal waters. Many products people use at home and in the yard—cleansers, paints, nail polishes, pesticides, and motor oils—contain toxic ingredients. When dumped on driveways, in streets, down storm drains, or down kitchen sinks, these chemicals can end up in streams and rivers, which lead to coastal waters. Waste treatment plants usually cannot get all the toxic pollutants out of the water before they release it into streams, bays, and the ocean. Check your local library for information on household toxins and alternatives to those toxins. Call your local sanitation department and ask them about household hazardous waste disposal programs in your area. You could also check the following publications for information:

Nontoxic, Natural, and Earthwise by Debra Lynn Dadd (Jeremy P. Tarcher, 1990).
Ranger Rick April 1988, a special Earth Day issue

For commercially prepared alternatives to toxic household products, contact Seventh Generation, listed above, or Real Goods, listed in the entry below.

- Turn off lights, televisions, and other appliances when you are not using them. Reduce unnecessary car trips by walking, bicycling, taking buses, or combining trips. Saving oil and gas and the electricity that may be made in power plants that burn oil and gas helps prevent the need for the offshore oil drilling and oil transport that can lead to oil spills and other ocean pollution. Encourage your family to use energy-saving devices in your home. For more energy-saving tips, contact your local electric utility. For a catalog of energy-saving appliances and other environmental products, write or call:

Real Goods
966 Mazzoni Street
Ukiah, CA 95482-3471
Phone 1-800-762-7325

- Write letters to state and national government officials, telling them you feel ocean conservation is important.

GLOSSARY

benthos   organisms that live in or on the ocean bottom

bioluminescence   light produced by living organisms by a chemical reaction. This light is produced without heat.

biome   an area that has a certain kind of community of plants and animals. In the case of terrestrial biomes, but not in aquatic biomes, they have a certain climate as well.

blubber   a thick, fatty layer that keeps the bodies of marine mammals warm

buoyancy   how high or low an object or animal floats in a fluid such as water

chemosynthetic bacteria   bacteria that produce their own food through a chemical reaction using sulfur from hydrothermal vents

circumpolar   circling one or both of the earth's poles

continental shelf   zone just offshore of an island or continent, stretching from the low-tide line to where the ocean floor begins to slope markedly

continental slope   zone beyond the continental shelf, where the ocean bottom begins a fairly steep descent into deeper water

current water that moves, usually long distances, through the ocean and whose movement is unrelated to tides

El Niño a pattern of weather systems that creates a warm current flowing south along the coast of Ecuador

elasmobranchs a class of fish who have skeletons made of cartilage. Sharks, rays, and skates are members of this class.

evaporate to change from a liquid into a gas

filter feed to strain small particles of food from water

gyre the large, circular ocean current produced by surface winds. The Atlantic and Pacific each have two gyres.

hydrothermal vent a vent in the ocean floor where superheated water spurts out. This water has been heated by percolating through volcanically heated rocks.

nekton ocean-dwelling animals that are active swimmers

nematocyst stinging cell used by a jellyfish to capture prey and defend itself

oceanographer a scientist who studies the ocean biome

plankton organisms that primarily float along with ocean currents instead of actively swimming

phyla the highest groupings of animals within the animal kingdom. Scientists group organisms according to the characteristics they share.

phytoplankton tiny, often microscopic, plants that float in the ocean

red tide an overgrowth of algae in the surface waters of the ocean. These algae may sometimes turn the water red.

The algae can also produce toxins that build up in fish and shellfish and may sicken or kill people who eat them.

salinity the concentration of salt dissolved in a liquid

sea a subdivision of the ocean. Seas are lobes of the ocean partly surrounded by land.

sea-floor spreading the process by which new ocean crust is formed at mid-ocean ridges

submersible a vehicle for underwater exploration

tide periodic rise and fall in the ocean water levels worldwide

trench a long, narrow, steep-sided depression in the ocean floor

tsunami a wave of great height caused by an earthquake or volcanic eruption underneath the ocean. Also called a seismic sea wave.

zooplankton tiny animals that travel through the ocean primarily by floating along with the currents. Zooplankton can include many types of animals such as copepods, jellyfish, worms, and the larvae of crabs and mollusks.

INDEX

PHOTO CREDITS